MUSHROOM SPIRIT
ORACLE

T0405432

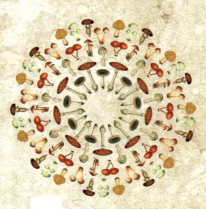

The greatest gift we can give ourselves is the power of observation.

Our teachers are all around us if we take the time to notice.

MUSHROOM SPIRIT

ORACLE

Nicola McIntosh

ROCKPOOL

A Rockpool book
PO Box 252
Summer Hill
NSW 2130
Australia

rockpoolpublishing.com

Follow us! f 🄾 rockpoolpublishing
Tag your images with #rockpoolpublishing

ISBN: 9781922785046

Published in 2023 by Rockpool Publishing
Copyright text © Nicola McIntosh, 2023
Copyright images © Nicola McIntosh, 2023
Copyright design © Rockpool Publishing, 2023

Design by Daniel Poole, Rockpool Publishing
Edited by Heather Millar

All rights reserved. No part of this publication may be
reproduced, stored in a retrieval system, or transmitted
in any form or by any means, electronic, mechanical,
photocopying, recording or otherwise, without the
prior written permission of the publisher.

Printed and bound in China
10 9 8 7 6 5 4 3 2

CONTENTS

INTRODUCTION

Welcome to the wonderful world of the mushroom. All mushrooms are classed as fungi; however, not all fungi are mushrooms. The mushroom is the fruiting body of what is called 'mycelium'. Mycelium can be likened to the roots of a tree, with the mushroom forming the tree itself. It forms a network underground that connects everything. When we see a ring of mushrooms, commonly known as fairy rings, we know that underneath the ground lies a disc of mycelium. Mycelium can stretch for miles; the largest one known to date measures close to 2,400 acres. It is a vast underground network connected to many tree roots and this helps trees to communicate with one another and everything can 'voice' what it needs. The mycelium then ensures the right nutrients are distributed where they are needed. It also reminds us that we are all connected.

Fungi is responsible for more than 90 per cent of decomposition around the world. Its function is to break down and redistribute nutrients from decomposing materials. This makes them gatekeepers between life and death. They decompose that which was once alive, allowing the physical parts to be recycled into something new.

The primary function of the mushroom is to help spread spores, enabling them to reproduce. They can release anywhere up to 7 trillion spores depending on which type they are. The spores then only grow when the conditions are right. Some are eaten and return to the lifecycle, and some will be lucky enough to grow.

Fungi may be close to 2 billion years old, existing here on earth well before plants and animals. They are incredibly complex and more closely resemble animals than plants. In fact, they sit in their own class. Fungi actually share close to 50 per cent of the DNA of humans and 85 per cent of our RNA, which explains why they have such an effect on the human body. Many remain mostly unknown to us — out of literally millions of fungi, only about 2–10 per cent of them have been classified, and out of that small percentage, only about 10 mushrooms are used medicinally.

There are many species of mushrooms, just like herbs and plants, so it is vitally important when collecting and using them to get the correct Latin name and understand the mushroom's distinguishing features so they can be properly identified.

Mushrooms go largely undetected from view, but without them, we would not survive. Certain mushrooms have relationships with particular trees, depending on the climate and soil, and this makes it easier for us to find them. Many medicinal mushrooms are now cultivated on a wide scale due to their increasing popularity, and this has created a more sustainable practice than wildcrafting (also known as foraging).

They have been here long before humans and are incredibly intelligent life-forms. We have much to learn from them and my hope is that this oracle deck starts your journey of discovery. Knowing that we can use them in our everyday lives opens up the possibility of working with them on more than just a spiritual level – for example, we can gain optimal physical health from medicinal varieties, which are easy to integrate into our lives.

Once you delve into the world of mushrooms, you will gain the utmost respect for their teachings. Powerful, ancient and wise, they carry the secrets of the earth we are still yet to uncover.

DISCLAIMER: Unless you are highly trained in the identification of mushrooms, please do not forage or harvest your own. If you are not 100 per cent certain of the identity of the mushroom, do not pick it. There are many lookalikes and eating the wrong one can lead to sickness and death. You can purchase medicinal and edible mushrooms from reputable sellers, so please play it safe.

You can also learn to cultivate many medicinal and edible mushrooms at home, and there are many good books and courses on the subject to get you started. I highly recommend any work by Paul Stamets if you are wanting to delve further, along with *Radical Mycology* by Peter McCoy, which is an incredibly in-depth book. And start off small – the world of mushrooms is like travelling down the rabbit hole!

How to use the Oracle

Doctrine of signatures

Given that we have only identified approximately 2–10 per cent of all mushrooms, there are many that we have no understanding of at all. So how do we understand the messages they have to show us? We use the doctrine of signatures. This doctrine has been widely used for centuries to help us better understand what a plant or herb can be used for by observing its colour, shape, location and growing conditions. Sometimes just the shape alone looks like the organ it can be used for, and the direction or colour of the flowers might indicate a particular plant or herb's use for a condition of the upper body. Sometimes the doctrine is a little difficult to see and sometimes can't be seen at all, but it is a good place to start and, in many cases, has been backed up with scientific validation over time.

When the doctrine is not immediately obvious, one might use a shamanic journey to connect with the mushroom spirit. Yes, that is a thing. The mushroom spirit would be from the entire mycelium underneath the ground, not just the fruiting body of the mushroom. We know mycelium networks are incredibly intelligent. They are able to place themselves exactly where they are needed to acquire what they need by forming relationships among certain trees, plants and even insects. They are able to break down an incredible array of substances and some can even break down plastic. The qualities possessed by the ones used medicinally are not matched by herbs or drugs. So what better way to communicate with this intelligence than by connecting spiritually and energetically with it?

If you wish to go deeper and experience the true connection of the mushrooms and mycelium, I suggest you either meditate with each card for a deeper connection, or if you are familiar with shamanic journeying, you can communicate with the mushroom via this method. There is no wrong or right way – use whatever feels right to you. In this way, you will not only connect more wholly with the deck, but you will also most likely gain a deeper understanding of each card and its specific messages for you. Don't be confined by the guidebook, it is just a place to start your journey.

The doctrine of signatures also helps us look at subjects more closely, and as is the case when using any oracle deck, imagery is key. Spirit communicates to us through the deck's images, so what you see in the image may communicate something other than what is described in the guidebook. Always trust your gut and use your intuition as you become more familiar with the oracle cards and the secret world of mushrooms.

You may like to keep a journal and number a page for each of the cards. When other meanings come to you, write them there. You will begin to develop a deeper relationship and connection with the cards and the mushroom network.

For more information about shamanism and the doctrine of signatures, check out my book *Plant Spirit Medicine* (Rockpool 2022).

How to start

Shuffle the deck and call in the mushroom spirits to be with you. I normally say, 'Mushroom spirits, please be with me now. I ask for your guidance.' When working with spirit, it's important to always be respectful, honest and trusting. Always ask permission beforehand, and afterwards thank the energies that work through the cards for you. The more you make this connection, the more you will receive from your oracle.

There is no right or wrong way to pick out your cards. Just pull them out of the deck any way you like. Go where you are drawn. If any cards fall out keep them aside because they will have meaning in your reading and provide some extra information spirit is trying to communicate to you. If I am reading for others, I allow them to shuffle the deck and pick their own cards, but you can also do this for them. When you trust that the right information will come through no matter what, you let go of the fear that something can be done wrong.

There are no hard and fast rules with the oracle, and there are quick and simple readings when you are a little time-poor.

You can pull one card a day to give you guidance on what to expect or what energy to be aware of for the day.

You can pull a card to meditate upon or undertake a shamanic journey with.

You can do a three-card spread, which may represent past, present and future.

For more in-depth readings, you may like to work with one of the following spreads, which I find incredibly powerful.

The obstacle spread

Draw four cards in the following sequence. You can tell spirit what each card represents before you pick them. This clearly communicates what you need to know before you are guided to select the card.

Card 1 represents where you are now.

Card 2 represents where you want to be.

Card 3 represents the steps needed to get where you want to be.

Card 4 represents the obstacles you might need to overcome to get there.

The mycelium spread

This spread gives you more information on contributing factors surrounding an issue that needs to be looked at.

Card 1 represents what lies beneath or is unseen that is an important base.

Card 2 represents what is needed to make things stable and grow.

Card 3 represents what it will look like when complete.

Card 4 represents any elements or relationships it relies on for growth.

Card 5 represents where it will eventually end and start anew.

These are merely examples of what you can do with the cards but let this be a guide. If you feel something else resonates with you, go with it. Be creative and make up your own spreads – there are no rules. Remember, the cards are communication tools for spirit to connect to you. Let your intuition guide you always.

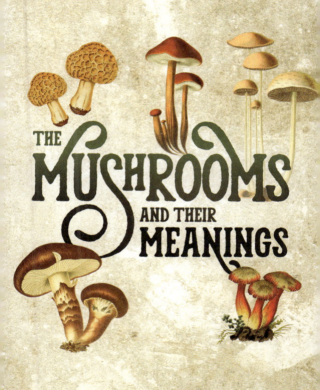

THE
MUSHROOMS
AND THEIR
MEANINGS

1

REISHI
spirit medicine
Ganoderma lucidum

EDIBLE / MEDICINAL

Reishi, known as the queen of mushrooms, is also one of the most well-known for its medicinal qualities. It has been used extensively in Chinese medicine for at least 2,000 years and is known as the mushroom of longevity and vitality. It is a powerful immune modulator, promotes good sleep, reduces stress and helps with allergies.

In Chinese, it is known as lingzhi or 'spirit herb' and is considered to be a bridge between heaven and earth. There are many types of reishi and all have similar qualities. In Chinese medicine, *G. lucidum* calms the spirit and nourishes the heart. Since your 'shen' or spirit resides in the heart, when your heart qi is weak, it cannot restrain the spirit from travelling up to your head, which in turn causes insomnia and restlessness. By nourishing the heart, you therefore calm the shen and it returns to the heart, where it can rest. Reishi is not only good for heart conditions, it also tones the lung qi, which aids in respiratory function. It is a powerful adaptogen, helping your body to adapt to stress and making it the perfect mushroom to aid in meditation.

You can find reishi on the lower parts of hardwood trees such as oak. It has a shiny appearance to it and can look fake.

Card meaning

Reishi is heart medicine – spirit medicine. Are you feeling unsettled and needing to bring calm into your life? Do you need to find what your spirit is searching for? Are you overthinking things and exhausting your heart qi, so your spirit is unsettled? Then it is time to ground yourself and nurture your spirit. Sit in your heart centre and see where you can start nurturing yourself better. Introducing reishi into your diet and spiritual practices may be needed at this time. It is time for calm on a spiritual level so it can filter down to the physical.

Reishi helps to nourish your mind, body and spirit (heart). It allows your body to rest and recover, while offering it the nourishment and support that it needs. This is a great lesson to learn for those who are overworked, stressed, not sleeping and continuing to push themselves. It is important to rest. It is important to bring meditation into your spiritual practices. Are you making time for your spiritual practices? How are you nourishing yourself? How are you nourishing your spirit? Only you can answer these questions.

Being able to nourish your shen or spirit is something that is not often seen in the herbal world, making reishi an exceptional medicine.

If the key to longevity and vitality is nourishing the spirit, shouldn't you be following what makes your heart and spirit sing? Reishi is reminding you it is time to create calm, to listen to what your spirit needs.

· 2 ·

Chaga
defence/balance

Chaga
defence/balance
Inonotus obliquus

EDIBLE / MEDICINAL

Chaga is quite an unusual-looking mushroom. It grows on the bark of living trees and is often mistaken for a tree burl or growth of some sort. It is commonly found on birch trees and its relationship with the black birch produces the highest quality chaga. It doesn't seem to like being cultivated, so when harvesting in the wild, care should be taken not to destroy the tree and some chaga should be left for it to grow back.

I. obliquus is also known as the king of mushrooms and rightly so. It is a superfood and its medicinal qualities are endless. It has one of the highest antioxidant levels in a food known to humans. Where acai berries – commonly thought of as a superfood – are 800 on the ORAC scale, chaga is up to 36,000. (The ORAC scale – oxygen radical absorbance capacity – measures a food's antioxidant value.)

Chaga is very nutrient dense. This may be due to its long lifespan of up to 20 years absorbing nutrients and the fact that birch water from inside the tree that it is taking its nutrients from is also highly nutrient dense. Let's also mention that chaga is considered to have potent anti-cancer and anti-tumour medicinal qualities, then take a look at the doctrine of signatures – the mushroom looks like a tumour or growth on the tree. It is also anti-allergic, anti-inflammatory, anti-hyperglycemic, anti-viral and anti-bacterial among other things.

Chaga is also extremely high in melanin, which helps protect the skin. Melanin aids in melatonin production, which aligns with circadian rhythms. This is why it can help you sleep. Another property of melatonin is to de-calcify your pineal gland – said to be where your third eye chakra is located – making chaga a spiritually aligning mushroom.

Card meaning

Chaga is the king when it comes to helping the body defend itself and ward off potential dangers to your health. Where in your life could you have something or someone attached to you that is not serving your higher purpose or is creating a hinderance of some sort? Is it time to build your defences so strong that nothing can penetrate them? Are you physically strong enough or do you need to work on your physical health? Maybe you are allowing yourself to be taken advantage of or are being treated poorly.

Sometimes when you feel you need protection, you actually need to strengthen your reserves. Using energy to block things and cast things away can be more tiring than building yourself up from the inside so nothing can stick to you.

Another lesson from chaga is one of balance. Disease exists when something in the body becomes unbalanced. Chaga brings balance to your immune system, blood sugar levels and circadian rhythms. Where are you out of spiritual alignment? It might be time to look at where something within you or your life is out of balance. Where can you create more flow and movement? Where have things become stuck? When you balance yourself from within, this balances your external world. The work you do on the inside can create profound shifts – if you are prepared to do the work. When you create balance and cultivate strength from the inside, you become an impenetrable force.

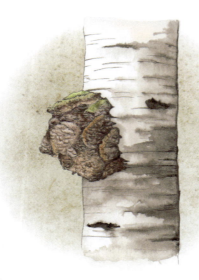

3

SHIITAKE
nourish
Lentinula edodes

EDIBLE / MEDICINAL

L. edodes grows on fallen tree branches and logs, making it popular for the home cultivator because pre-inoculated logs can be purchased to place in your backyard. The logs can produce mushrooms for up to six years, serving as a food and medicine.

Shiitake is nutritious and a good substitute for meat. High in amino acids, copper, zinc and B vitamins, shiitake – if grown under specific UV lights or sun-dried – can have a staggering amount of vitamin D. It is a powerful immune activator, may reduce blood pressure, fight cancer, give energy, support healthy hair and skin, decrease inflammation, and lower cholesterol. Traditional Chinese texts refer to *L. edodes* as the 'elixir of life'. It is known to tone qi and blood.

Card meaning

Something or someone in your life needs nourishment. Nourishment comes in many forms, from the food you eat to the things that make your heart sing. Are you replacing the energy you are expending or are you becoming worn out? Are you attending to your garden? And to your inside environment as well as your internal?

You cannot completely nourish your soul if you are starving somewhere else in your life. Are you yearning for something? Is there a hole that needs filling or a project that needs more attention given to it? Take stock of the areas of your life that need more nourishment. Whether physical, emotional, spiritual, mental or creative, make a note of what needs more attention in your life and nourish it. Maybe you need to put more nourishment into your relationships with people, pets, plants or yourself. Ask yourself, 'Who or what is missing out? What can I give more of?'

Is there a project you have started that needs more of your attention? Every project that is started and not finished still holds a part of your energy attached to it. It may be time to complete all those unfinished projects and nourish what you started to completion.

If you don't know where to start, nourish yourself in such a way that you know how to. When you notice where the gaps in your life are, you can take action to change them, making you feel more whole.

4

TURKEY TAIL
======

block

Trametes versicolor

EDIBLE / MEDICINAL

Known for its many striking colours and turkey tail-like shape, the turkey tail mushroom is common all around the world. It has many health benefits but is most commonly known for its immune-enhancing abilities. Studies have proven *T. versicolor* to be effective in the treatment of cancer and it is often used alongside chemotherapy. Turkey tail contains compounds called polysaccharides that appear to inhibit growth of cancer cells and stimulate the immune system.

Card meaning

Where is there a blockage or stagnation in your life? It is time to focus on building your energy and defences so you can shift this stuck energy. Chinese medicine says, if there is debris in a creek causing it to be blocked, do not lift each heavy piece out of the way individually; instead, build the flow of water, so its force moves the debris on effortlessly. The creek or river is our blood and qi, and the debris is stuck energy, repressed emotions and the accumulation of fluids that need movement to transform them. When we build ourselves up on the inside, we give ourselves a better chance of pushing through obstacles within and outside of ourselves.

Turkey tail is effective in cancer treatment. Cancer is the proliferation of cells in an abnormal state – that is, an overgrowth of cells. Ask yourself, 'What has triggered something in my life to grow out of control and dangerously?' Is something you have left unchecked grown to a point that it is no longer serving you? Or is there someone or something in your life that is no longer for your highest good? It is time to look around you and inside yourself to find what stands in the way of your flow and remove it. By making this stand and strengthening your energy, you allow the life force that moves you to flow naturally, bringing balance and harmony back to your life.

5

LIONS MANE
calm
Hericium erinaceus

EDIBLE / MEDICINAL

Lions mane mushrooms are beautiful white roundish fungi with a shaggy or hairy appearance. Both edible and medicinal, lions mane offers a wide array of benefits including improving cognitive and heart health, reducing inflammation, improving the immune system and restoring the nervous system. The doctrine of signatures is strong with this one – the mane of *H. erinaceus* looks like the many fibres of the nervous system.

Card meaning

Your cognitive function and nervous system are intrinsically linked. When you are under stress, both are affected. When one is calmed, so is the other.

26

It is hard to operate at your peak mentally and physically when you are under chronic stress. You may find things harder to do and you are more likely to make mistakes since your body is in fight or flight mode. If you are to make more grounded decisions and perform tasks more effectively, you need to calm your nervous system and take care of yourself. When your body says it is tired, it means it needs rest or nutrition, not caffeine and sugar. If you keep adding stimulants, you keep yourself on edge and in fight or flight mode. When you listen to your body and what it needs, you can then understand why you have the highs and lows, and why you need to look after your nervous system.

Where do you hold your tension? Why do you hold your tension? What are your triggers and what do you do to eliminate or help your body out of stress mode? If you are to have a healthy mindset, it is important to look after the nutrition you feed it, the lifestyle you live and the practices you incorporate. Sustainability is all about pace. Remember the tortoise and the hare? Be the tortoise and pace yourself. Slow and steady wins the race. Don't burn yourself out.

6

MAITAKE
celebrate
Grifola frondosa

EDIBLE / MEDICINAL

Maitake is also known as hen of the woods, because of its feathered bottom–like appearance. Maitake is the Japanese name for 'dancing mushroom'. Apparently, people danced for joy when they found it. *G. frondosa* grows at the base of maple, oak or elm trees, and can grow very large. It has an earthy flavour and can be used in any food dish or as a medicinal extract. It is known to help regulate blood sugar levels and lower cholesterol. Maitake is a powerful adaptogen, and can help the body to adapt and recover from stress.

Card meaning

It's time to celebrate – something you have been working towards is nearing completion. All your hard work will pay off and this could be the start of something new. Whatever this celebration means to you, this card is one of the most positive and auspicious in the whole deck.

A sense of achievement is a beautiful feeling and something you can be proud of, so remember to celebrate your wins, no matter how small. Knowing how much you have achieved should make you feel proud; understand there is no need to look for external gratification to show you your self-worth.

When we feel we have achieved something great, this shines from within, so allow yourself this time to shine. Do not feel you need to dull your shine to make others around you feel good. Celebrate, and let those who truly care for you celebrate as well, because you are glowing. Dance for joy, knowing that because of this achievement a new beginning is on the horizon.

You might dance for joy when you finally find something you've been looking or hoping for. This could mean a new job, a partner or a pet. Many things in life should be celebrated and it is important to keep that celebratory joy flowing. Once it is here, nurture it, don't let it go unnoticed. Always remember how important it is to you.

7

CORDYCEPS
essence
Cordyceps militaris

EDIBLE / MEDICINAL

Cordyceps is a unique mushroom because it generally needs an insect as a host to fruit. It attacks the host, then replaces the tissue and sprouts from inside its body. The insect is sometimes referred to as a zombie host. The insect, as well as the fungi, have been used in Chinese medicine for centuries.

There are many types of cordyceps, but the two main ones used for medicine are *C. sinensis* and *C. militaris*. *C. sinensis* comes from the high altitude of Tibet and has been extensively harvested, which has given rise to the question of its sustainability. *C. militaris* is used as a replacement and after extensive research is now able to be cultivated, without the use of insects, in a sustainable way.

Cordyceps in Chinese medicine gently tones the kidney yang (fire/heat), builds the essence, tonifies the lungs and settles coughs. It is classed as sweet and warm, and because it tones both yin and yang, it is seen as a harmonious tonic. It is gentle in its actions and therefore can be used long term.

From a Western perspective, cordyceps is widely known to help people perform better athletically. It is known to increase energy and help with lung conditions such as asthma. For this reason, it is becoming increasingly popular now in the West.

Card meaning

What do you need to excel? Do you need help from someone or something? Do you need that extra push to help you grow? It might be time to take what you need to give you the strength and stamina to get to where you need to be. Are you looking after yourself? Are you replacing the stores that you use, or are you burning yourself out? It's time to look inwards and ask yourself, 'What do I need? Do I need to be a bit selfish and put all my time and energy into me?' There are lots of questions here.

The other point this card might be making is that there may be someone or something that is sucking your energy from you. You may be the mushroom – or are you the insect in this case? Who or what is draining you of your energy so that you cannot grow to your full potential? Is someone else taking the limelight while you have done all the work, or vice versa?

Cordyceps is asking you to find that inner strength and life force to help push you forward, to keep you alive and flourishing. Don't allow others to sponge from you and take your essence. Alternatively, find what you need from someone or something to help you succeed, but make sure it is done in a sustainable way so it doesn't have a negative impact on anyone. Look at the areas in your life where you can grow, find a project that can help you achieve this, or find a relationship that will help you find the results you seek.

8

ENOKI
align
Flammulina filiformis

EDIBLE / MEDICINAL

Native to China, Japan and Korea, the enoki is a well-known mushroom and the white, thin-stalked one in grocery stores is the cultivated variety. Enoki can also be found in the wild, but it is generally thicker and is brown and yellow. *F. filiformis* is commonly used in Asian dishes and is a low-calorie, high-protein mushroom packed full of nutrients and fibre. As well as having excellent nutritional value, the enoki shares the same properties as many medicinal mushrooms, in that it is immune enhancing, has anti-cancer and anti-aging qualities, lowers high blood pressure, and balances blood sugar levels.

Card meaning

Together we stand tall. A single enoki mushroom is thin and weak, but when grown together, it is tall and strong. Grown together, enoki are all the same, just varying sizes, and together they are something significant.

Sometimes strength comes in numbers and also in finding your tribe. When we align our values and morals with others, we can make more of a difference than we can alone. We are becoming ever more aware of the power of group consciousness and community. What may seem unsurmountable at first can be conquered together. Whether with just one other person or many, it is time to feel empowered and strong, knowing that the relationships we form have the ability to make massive changes in our lives, the lives of others and the planet itself.

Who can you align with to help with your projects and dreams? Where can you offer help to others who want to achieve the same as yourself? What do you bring to the table? What are your gifts that, when combined with like-minded people, can elevate what you are trying to achieve? When we work in this manner with our tribe or community, the combined energy is a powerful force. Ensure that you are using this force with all the right intentions.

Who can you align with to help you achieve success and make positive change? Stand tall, grow together and support one another.

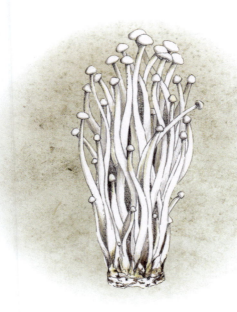

9

OYSTER
regeneration
Pleurotus ostreatus

`EDIBLE`

OYSTER
regeneration

Oyster mushroom feeds on dead or decaying matter, mostly wood, so you will find it grows in clusters known as shelves, on or near trees. It forms a relationship with deciduous trees such as oak and beech, and tends to grow in the shade in leafy forests. It is also heavily cultivated due to the fact it is one of the most consumed mushrooms in the world. *P. ostreatus* comes in a few different colours, is easy to grow and grows very fast, making it the perfect mushroom to grow yourself. New research is also being undertaken around its ability to clean up toxins in the environment, such as oil spills.

Card meaning

The oyster mushroom grows rapidly and is prolific in many areas, so this card indicates a time of rapid growth or movement. The oyster mushroom has many benefits, which is why it is used so widely. This could spell a time of great growth for you, for others or for a project you are working on. Whatever it is, everything and every one has a purpose, no matter how big or small.

It may also be a time to let go of something that is dying anyway. When you let go of 'dead wood', you create room for new things to grow. You may not realise how fast this shift can happen but know that, when you make the decision to let go, this is when growth begins. From the old, the new is built.

Everything is recycled. This is the cycle of life – building on what is already there, so you don't need to start from the beginning. Break down what you need and what you don't need; cultivate growth from old ways and construct the new with these tools.

Whatever in your life this card is relating to, know that it will happen fast, and it will have an important part to play. It's not about re-inventing the wheel, it's about using what you already know works.

TREMELLA
yin
Tremella fuciformis

EDIBLE

Also known as snow fungus, silver ear or the beauty mushroom, *T. fuciformis* has a gelatinous look to it and is classed as a jelly fungus. It eats other fungi, unlike most mushrooms, which like to consume decaying wood. It is also full of vitamin D and antioxidants, and is anti-inflammatory like many other mushrooms.

Tremella has many benefits including stimulating hyaluronic acid in the skin, which declines with age. It draws moisture to the skin, making it highly beneficial in skin care. It is able to hold approximately 500 times its own weight in water, which makes it of great use in restoring yin or fluids within the body. In Chinese medicine, it is well-known for helping with the lungs, which govern the skin. It's good for dry coughs and calming the stomach. Tremella is well-known as the beauty mushroom.

Card meaning

The key word here is yin. Tremella is shown to help with the yin aspect of the body. Within the yin and yang concept, yin is the opposite of yang. Yin is fluid, cold, calm, nurturing, descending, whereas yang is fire, fast, ascending, controlling. When one is out of balance, so will the other be because they need each other for balance. This card is therefore saying it is time to bring more yin into your life. Where are you out of balance? Where has the yang/masculine taken control? Where can you take your hands off the steering wheel and fall into flow? Take time to nurture yourself and slow down.

There are many ways you can bring yin into your life: drink more water and less caffeine; do yin yoga, slow stretching or meditation; eat nourishing non-spicy foods; take a bath; or walk in the water. If left unchecked, yang can take control and then it will exhaust itself. The yin will be exhausted also, leaving your whole body in deficit.

Being the beauty mushroom, tremella may also be asking you what you are showing to the world. Are you feeling vibrant within yourself or are you feeling depleted? What do you need to fill your cup and shine from the inside? Only you will know what you need, so it is you who needs to make the changes. Become soft like this jelly-looking mushroom. There is beauty in softness as well as beauty in restoration.

11

KING OYSTER
substance
Pleurotus eryngii

EDIBLE

The king oyster mushroom is known by many names – king brown and king trumpet among others – and is easily identifiable with its thick stem and dark brown cap. Like most edible mushrooms, *P. eryngii* is nutrient dense, high in fibre and protein, and low in calories. It has similar amazing anti-inflammatory properties, as well as possibly lowering cholesterol, improving the immune system and having anti-cancer properties. It is also high in antioxidants and has the longest shelf life of all the oyster mushrooms. Found wild in southern Europe and North Africa, it has been cultivated and used for some time in China, Japan and Italy, and is the longest lasting of the oyster mushrooms.

Card meaning

The king oyster mushroom is large and meaty. For this reason, it is often used as a substitute for meat in meals. It is thick and full bodied, with many health benefits. In drawing the king oyster card, you are being called to look at where you can substitute something you currently use for something that will give you more value. Where can you beef something up with an alternative? Is there another way to do something that will create more value in what you are doing?

The king oyster is about substance. There are many things you can use in place of others and finding something with substance as well as relevance is key here. The king is indeed very big and can make a complete meal with a single mushroom. Show that you have substance, show that you can stand alone, because you are enough by yourself. Show that you have amazing qualities without the use of anything else. Stand in your power and be a leader.

Look for quality and substance in everything you do and the people you choose to let into your life. Substance is about giving back, how you can help and focus on making something purposeful.

42

12

MOREL
restore
Morchella esculenta

`EDIBLE`

The morel mushroom is highly prized for its unique savoury flavour and known for its unusual sponge-like shape. It is usually found in abundance around the base of hardwood trees, such as oak, elm, ash and aspen. There are many different types of morels and only some have been able to be cultivated, making the foraged ones a rarity. *M. esculenta* must always be eaten cooked, or it may cause stomach upset. It is one of the highest sources of vitamin D of the edible mushrooms, with shiitake being the highest when dried under specific light conditions. It is completely hollow from the base to the tip inside, which distinguishes it from poisonous lookalikes. In Chinese medicine, it is highly prized for its tonic qualities and is often made into nourishing soups.

Card meaning

Drawing the morel could mean that it's time to restore and build yourself up from the inside. Have you become empty inside? Do you feel like something is missing from your life? Are you feeling completely drained and like you have given too much of yourself? It is time to enjoy the wonderful energy that morel brings.

It's hard for people to see inside to understand if you are feeling weary, depleted or depressed. It is a time to take matters into your own hands, look inwards and work at restoring and building yourself up. Perceptions can sometimes be wrong. Don't underestimate what may be going on underneath someone's seemingly fine exterior. The intricacy of the exterior of the morel is the complete opposite to what is inside, so don't let your first impression fool you.

Do what brings you joy. Eat and be merry. Exercise or sit under a tree in the sun. Create or take up a hobby that's always been on your list. The time is now and only you know how to fill that void. It may also be someone you know or something that needs attention. Whatever the case may be, attend to their essential needs – these might not be obvious. Look deeper to understand what is missing and what can be gained and how you can help. Reach out if you need to, because no-one can see under the surface better than yourself. It's time to find nourishment.

13

Common Puffball

let go

Lycoperdon perlatum

EDIBLE

Mainly found in woodlands and grasslands, the common puffball is a spiky-looking mushroom that is edible until it is mature. When mature, a small hole forms in the top, allowing its cloud of spores to be dispersed. When you slice a puffball in half, it should be white all the way through, with no gills inside. Amanita mushrooms (fly agaric and death cap) look similar when young, but they have gills inside when cut and death caps have a slight olive tinge to them, so they are not to be confused with puffballs.

Card meaning

The puffball mushroom is a reminder to let go. As it releases its spores in a cloud, it reminds you to exhale.

What are you holding onto that you need to let out? What needs to be let go of to put down roots and grow somewhere differently? Have you been holding on too tightly to something or just waiting for exactly the right moment to let it go?

It may be a time to set the wheels in motion because the timing is right or it may be asking you to wait until the time is right. Remember that all the steps must be followed for the letting go to be as effective as possible.

Puffball may be calling to you to speak something into being. Words and intentions are powerful creative forces. When you are present and make your intentions or desires known, you start an energy flow to manifest them. Just like the spores that float away and grow exactly where they land, so too do your words and intentions go where they are needed.

When the exhale is over and you have let go of what was needed somewhere else, you create an ending of sorts and a beginning of something new. Everything is in divine timing. Nothing is rushed and everything is as it is meant to be.

14

AMETHYST DECEIVER
deception

Laccaria amethystina

EDIBLE

(though can contain high levels of
arsenic if present in the soil)

Found in leaf litter in woodlands and under beech trees, the amethyst deceiver is an amazing violet colour, which during wet weather will show a deep purple. During dry weather and when it matures, the cap changes to a very pale, almost white colour, making *L. amethystina* look similar to other mushrooms that can be poisonous.

Card meaning

The deceiver mushroom comes to let you know that things may not be what they seem. You may be seeing things the wrong way, or there is deceit of some kind appearing before you. Not all deceit is bad – it can be a blessing in disguise and it may not be a conscious thing. Are you deceiving yourself about something? Are you not allowing yourself to see what is right in front of you because you haven't taken the time to truly see it? Or do you not want to see it?

This card is like a trickster; it can talk to you in riddles but at the same time make you face the reality of what is not seen.

Is there a person or issue in your life that keeps changing like a chameleon? Or something that you have perceived wrongly? Take a closer look. What puzzles you about the situation? Is your logic saying one thing and your intuition another? Let your intuition be your guide always. When things appear to be one thing but are actually another, your intuition will know. Your intuition is your soul compass. Trust it implicitly.

Sometimes assumptions are made about people or situations, and this can come from a limited understanding or lack of interest in really getting to know more. Take the time to really observe and research the situation until you are 100 per cent sure of what you are looking at. Don't let looks be deceiving.

15

GOLDEN TEACHER (MAGIC MUSHROOM)

introspection

Psilocybe cubensis

PSYCHEDELIC

Golden teacher is a hallucinogenic mushroom widely known throughout the world and is a cultivated strain of *P. cubensis*. Psilocybin is the main psychoactive component, and it is being studied for its effects on people with psychological disorders such as depression. Misidentification can be deadly. Golden teacher grows slower than other species but develops more psilocybin over this time. It is known for its introspective and philosophical effects, rather than just a trip like some other psychedelic mushrooms. When bruised or picked, it turns a blue colour, which is one way to identify it. In many countries, it is illegal.

Card meaning

When the student is ready, the teacher will appear. This is a time to expand your awareness by going within – for the teacher might actually be you. When you turn your attention inwards through meditation and stillness, you are able to connect to realms beyond your imagination.

In shamanism, practitioners can access the three worlds – upper, middle and lower – by journeying, which is like a form of meditation. Within each plane of existence, you can communicate with practically anything and anyone without the limits of time and distance. This is why you contain the whole universe inside you, and why you are your own best teacher.

The golden teacher mushroom is said to have a mild potency and is therefore good for beginners. This may be an indication you are at the beginning of your studies or to take your time slowly with something. Mild is the key word here. There is no need to do anything in excess. You can gain the answers you seek through some of the smallest acts.

Golden teachers may be used for enlightenment, but they also teach you to obtain the same level of consciousness without them. They are here to show you what you are capable of and how to break through the limits you place on yourself that keep you stuck in your physical reality. It is time to see beyond linear time and space and realise the potential you have within.

16

AMANITA
expanded awareness
Amanita muscaria

PSYCHEDELIC / POISONOUS

The amanita mushroom is an easy one to identify with its distinguishable red cap and white spots. It is mainly found in the northern hemisphere in the UK, North America, Europe, Siberia and Asia, but has been introduced to New Zealand, Australia, South Africa and South America. It is mostly found beneath pine trees in woodlands and has thus become a favourite of fairy tales and magick.

Considered poisonous due to its psychoactive alkaloid content, *A. muscaria* is commonly used for its strong psychedelic effects in shamanic and indigenous ceremonies. Siberian shamans noticed that reindeer became intoxicated by the amanita mushroom, so they would either kill them and eat their meat or drink their urine, because the alkaloids remained intact and they could get the effects of the psychoactive content in this way. They would also prepare the mushrooms in other ways and found that by drying them first, the effects could be increased. These alkaloids also make the mushroom a good insecticide, and placed in milk it will kill flies, hence it is also known by the name 'fly agaric'.

The fly agaric mushroom may in fact be where the story of Santa and his flying reindeer came from, including why he hails from the North Pole and wears red and white.

Card meaning

Because *A. muscaria* is used to alter your consciousness to help you access other planes of existence, this card represents the need to raise your consciousness to a higher level. It is time to see things from a higher and less physical perspective and a time of spiritual growth. It is time to rise up and let go of the restraints that keep you thinking inside the square. It is also time to think and see things completely differently.

The amanita does not decompose what it rises from, which is unusual for a mushroom. This is most likely due to its relationship with the pine tree, where what it once used to do is no longer required. Have you formed a relationship with something or someone where something you used to do is no longer necessary? What is your purpose now? Are you needing to look at the value you offer in a relationship and see where you both work together, or is it more of a one-sided feeling?

Red is also a colour that usually spells out danger. Eating amanita is not recommended, so this card may be a sign of something to look out for. A warning that you shouldn't partake of something unless it is done in the right manner and for the right reasons.

Anything can be a poison if not used properly or not handled with respect. Tread carefully and keep an open mind.

17

GHOST MUSHROOM
shine
Omphalotus nidiformis

INEDIBLE / POISONOUS

The ghost mushroom is native to southern Australia and is quite a large, bioluminescent fungus that glows a beautiful neon green in the dark. During the daytime, it is a cream colour and forms in the shape of a fan or tube-like structure and can have purple or a darkish colour in the middle. It resembles the oyster mushroom but is toxic and will cause vomiting if eaten. It forms at the base of living or decaying trees. It spends 99 per cent of its time underground, only fruiting once a year in mid-autumn, and it is highly poisonous.

The bioluminescence is created from a reaction with an enzyme and oxygen, meaning it makes its own light. This light is used to attract insects, which is essential to spread its spores to help *O. nidiformis* colonise new areas of the forest and ensure its survival.

Card meaning

Ghost mushroom reminds you that you need to wait until the time is right to appear or ask for help. You can keep doing what you need to do in the background without others, but at some stage you need to show yourself and work together with not only your tribe, but others who can help you grow or get you to where you need to go.

You cannot be seen if you shrink away from the outside world. Take the time to gather the necessary strength and many things you might need to take you to the next level. It doesn't matter how long it takes to get this done, just remember the five 'Ps': proper planning prevents poor performance. When you have planned and prepared everything well, the execution of the plan should work smoothly.

Another meaning of this card is to shine bright. Light up the room, make yourself seen – there is nothing wrong with shining brightly. Don't dull your shine for others; we are not here to play small. Find your tribe and shine together for a great cause.

Remember that we can all do our bit individually, but everyone doing their bit together is a powerful force. Light the way for others to follow, spread the beauty, grow and expand.

18

BLUE PINKGILL
rarity
Entoloma hochstetteri

INEDIBLE / POISONOUS

Featuring on the New Zealand $50 note is the blue pinkgill, a small blue mushroom native to the country. It can be found in forests throughout New Zealand, residing among the leaf litter of broadleaf or podocarp trees. With such a distinctive cobalt blue, it is truly a sight to see.

Blue in nature is a rare sight and blue pigment even rarer. Plants don't normally exhibit blue in nature and generally have no blue pigment in them to create the blue colour. The colour is created by their structure, which reflects the blue light wave giving the impression it is blue.

Blue pinkgill on the other hand actually has three azulene pigments that make up its stunning colour.

Scientists are not sure why the mushroom needs to be blue, because generally everything has a reason. It seems *E. hochstetteri* has chosen blue for a reason we are yet to determine. It may be that herbivores are not attracted to blue and therefore leave the mushrooms alone, but there may be other reasons.

Card meaning

Being a rarity doesn't necessarily mean that people fail to notice you. In fact, it can be quite the opposite, as seen in the blue pinkgill. Standing out can be beautiful when you look different from everything around you. Everyone serves a purpose, even if you don't understand what it is yet. Your purpose may be big, it may be small, but size doesn't equate to bigger and better. The simple act of seeing the beauty in what is in front of you has an effect on the larger scale.

Do you know what your purpose is? Do you see the beauty in your rarity? For there are incredibly complex pieces that make up your whole. Rarity is beautiful and rarity is not always unique; there will always be others just like you, so you can still find your tribe. By being rare, you deter what you don't want finding you. You stand untouched by those who would normally try to take you down. You go unnoticed to some but noticed to others.

Blue was always a hard colour to come by in olden days and therefore something only royalty could obtain. What is your uniqueness and how can you utilise it to stand out in a sea of the same? Stand tall and proud and enjoy being something special.

19

Death cap
endings
Amanita phalloides

INEDIBLE / POISONOUS

The death cap mushroom is so highly poisonous, one mushroom can kill an adult, and it is responsible for most deaths related to eating mushrooms. There is no way to remove the poison, even through cooking. The cap of *A. phalloides* is usually a pale green to yellow but can sometimes be white. It has white gills, a cup-like volva at the bottom and a high skirt ring, which are good distinguishing elements. It may have a slight ammonia smell to it and likes to establish itself near oak trees during warm, wet autumn weather.

Card meaning

Death cap is a sign of endings, whether coming or already here. Death can sometimes feel like a negative thing, but death represents new beginnings too. Letting go of that which no longer serves you can feel very painful, and it may be that something you have held onto isn't allowing you to move forward. Endings can also mean many positive things, especially if it means there is an end in sight for something you have been working on or are trying to achieve.

This card is a blessing, but also a warning. Don't be alarmed and don't let fear or negativity in; everything is as it should be. Know that there are greater things at work here. Don't resist what is coming – it is time to take your hands off the steering wheel and let what needs to fall away do so. Death always comes sooner or later and resisting just delays the process. But with death comes new life. The death of something gives you the building materials to start the new. What do you need to finish or bring to an end? What are you hoping will stop? Ask yourself, 'What do I need to let go of to bring what I desire into my life?' Make it final and remember RIP is rest in *peace*. Let go and let flow. Welcome a new start and go forth knowing it is for the greater good.

20

SCARLET ELF CUP

healing

Sarcoscypha coccinea

EDIBLE

Found on leaf litter, dead wood, in deciduous woodlands and by streams, the scarlet elf cup is a stunning mushroom with a distinctive red cup and short stem. The ruby elf cup is strikingly similar and hard to tell apart, but both are edible, so misidentification is not an issue. *S. coccinea* grows in winter and can be found all around the world. European folklore says that wood elves would drink their morning dew from the cups. Native Americans used it to stop bleeding and promote healing of wounds. A distinct doctor of signatures here.

Card meaning

A time of healing is here or on its way. The scarlet elf cup heals fresh wounds, whether physical, emotional or spiritual. Will you drink from its cup? The wounds you carry may be fresh, but everything can be healed given time. Be patient, but also make sure you don't let the wound stay open and fresh. Not only will you lose energy from this, but you will stay stationary until the gap is closed. You can't fill yourself with what you need or move forward if there is a leak.

Where are you losing energy? Where are you letting your wounds stay open? You can learn to grow and heal when you take the time to understand the lesson. Once the lesson is learned, you no longer need to keep repeating the pattern. So, if you are stuck in a repeating pattern that you can't seem to break, ask yourself, 'What do I need to learn from this?' When we start to look at the world and people as teachers, we move from victim to student. Look at situations without the emotional charge and see from a higher perspective.

Scarlet elf cup may also be asking us to help heal the wounds of others. Are you feeling called to service? Are there bridges that need mending? Where can you create healing in your life and with those around you? Every random act of kindness has incredible healing properties.

21

SHAGGY INK CAP
growth/destruction cycle

SHAGGY INK CAP
growth/destruction
cycle

Coprinus comatus

EDIBLE

(when young, white and fresh)

The shaggy ink cap can be found in grasslands and open woodlands and has various stages of growth. Initially it begins as a white egg-shape, growing into a long bell. The pale brown area at the top breaks into large scales and in dry weather the whole cap will do this. The gills start off white and turn to pink and then black. *C. comatus* will then deliquesce – that is, liquify or self-decompose – from the bottom outside edge and work its way upwards. Within a few hours, just a stem and small disc will remain. The stem is hollow and the stem ring will eventually become movable, often falling to the ground.

The shaggy ink cap is also a bioaccumulator of heavy metals, meaning it can clean up soil and restore its pH by drawing the heavy metals up into its fruiting body.

Card meaning

Each stage of your growth has different meanings and properties. Just like the shaggy ink cap, you go through many stages over and over again. Just like the earth has its seasons, every cycle has a purpose and needs to be worked with, not against. At what stage of your evolutionary growth are you? Can you recognise if it's a growth or destructive cycle? The shaggy ink cap has both and both are necessary.

When you look at a destructive cycle within yourself, do you try to push it away because you think it is bad? Or do you try to learn from it because it is a necessary part of growing up or learning a lesson? Not everything is bad when it is destructive and not everything that is growth is a good thing. When something grows or is destroyed, it must be a sustainable process or there is no balance. What can you keep in check before it grows out of control?

The key here is about finding balance within both the destructive and growth cycles. Remember that not everything destructive is bad and not everything that grows is good and vice versa. Everything has its place and purpose. Our job is to learn and grow from everything and everyone in our lives. What can you learn from this experience? A special card indeed with many questions to ponder.

22

Fairy inkcap

subtlety

Coprinellus disseminatus

EDIBLE

(but fragile and insubstantial)

The fairy inkcap is normally found in dense masses attached to tree stumps and roots. It starts off a pale white and turns to grey before it blackens and dies. Very delicate, *C. disseminatus* will collapse when touched in an absolutely stunning display if you ever come across them.

Card meaning

Some things can come and go in the blink of an eye. One day they are there, and the next they are gone. The energy here is delicate and fairy-like. This subtle energy is here to create a magickal atmosphere – a beauty that sometimes goes unseen. Are you noticing the subtle energies around you or are you too busy to notice? Fairy inkcap reminds you that many small or subtle acts can create massive shifts.

This card is a reminder to be subtle. Moving in on something like a steamroller might not be the right course of action. Subtlety is key here and can be extremely powerful, so give it a try. Someone may be trying to tell you something that you are not hearing because it is very subtle.

Much wisdom can be gained by observing and feeling the subtle energy around you. Every plant, tree or flower is giving off subtle energy. People, pets and places may have a subtle energy that can only be felt when you quiet yourself enough to be able to sense it. Fairy inkcap says to slow down, create stillness and mindfulness in your practices and you will gain great wisdom from the energies around you. You don't need to go out and search for this energy, it will find you if it hasn't already. But be ready to listen and take it on board because it could come and go before you even realise it.

23

WRINKLED PEACH MUSHROOM
unique

WRINKLED PEACH MUSHROOM
unique

Rhodotus palmatus

INEDIBLE

Unlike other mushrooms, *Rhodotus* is the only species of its kind, so it cannot be mistaken for any other mushroom. Basically, taxonomists found it hard to fit it into a category, so it was given its own. The cap has a rubbery feel to it and is near impossible to tear apart. Red or orange droplets cover the stem, which is a phenomenon known as guttation, and it is unclear why this occurs. Its food source is rotting elm wood, and with the decline of these trees, we now see less and less of these stunning mushrooms. *R. palmatus* can grow on other hardwoods, and it is listed on the International Union for Conservation of Nature (IUCN) Red List, meaning that it is endangered, and you cannot pick it.

Card meaning

This is a mushroom that represents something so unique, it is in its own class. This may represent you, someone you know or something you are working on, something so stunning that you can't put it into a category. Unique can also be rare – and with rarity there can also be obstacles. Just as the wrinkled peach mushroom has become scarce due to the lack of elm trees, so too could you become obsolete if your sustenance or support runs out.

Being unique obviously has its plus side as well, because with rarity comes a need to protect it, so it doesn't disappear. Unique minds and people are way-showers and can change the world. They are sometimes outcast for not conforming or being the same as the rest of the crowd, but when their beauty or wisdom is seen, they become noticeable for all the right reasons.

Being unique takes strength to stand on your own, to make your own path and not bend to peer pressure. Uniqueness is a strength, not a disability or weakness. Find what makes you unique and stand fully in your power. The world doesn't need more vanilla; it needs way-showers and creativity to change how we see and do things. Uniqueness is a gift – make sure you use it well. Bring what makes you, you, into everything you do, and you will draw to you the people who resonate with that energy. That is your unique medicine.

24

BAMBOO MUSHROOM
fertility
Phallus indusiatus

EDIBLE

Also known as veiled lady or long net stinkhorn, this amazing mushroom starts off from what looks like an underground egg. Once mature, the cap is covered in gleba – a solid mass of spores with a terrible smell – which classes this mushroom as a stinkhorn. The smell attracts flying insects that eat the gleba and get the spores stuck on them, which they then spread. What is truly remarkable is the veil will always just reach the ground and go no further and won't stop just before it. This net gives crawling insects on the forest floor an avenue to climb to the top to also help with dispersing the mushroom spores. *P. indusiatus* is a tropical stinkhorn and once the gleba has been completely consumed, the veil will be short-lived.

It is commonly found in China growing at the bottom of bamboo; hence it is also known as bamboo fungus and used in many Chinese food dishes. It is said to assist with inflammation, fever and heat conditions.

Card meaning

As its Latin name *Phallus indusiatus* implies, the centre of the bamboo mushroom looks *phallic*. This stinkhorn mushroom is good at what it does and that is all about spreading its spores as widely as possible. This card represents having a thorough understanding of what is necessary to achieve what you need to grow and spread your seeds.

Drawing this card suggests that, if you set the scene right by understanding the relationships you rely on, everything will come to you effortlessly to ensure your survival and spread your seeds. When you rely on others, you must understand their needs as much as your own to make any mutual relationship work. What you offer must be enticing and without having to do too much more, others will spread the word because you have laid the foundations right.

Being in relationships with other people can help you achieve and grow in ways that you necessarily can't on your own. The net you scatter is not to catch people; it is to help them get to where they want to be. You can show them how to overcome their obstacles and in return they help you overcome yours.

Drawing the fertility card indicates that something is about to spread and grow through the help of others, or it may be you who is helping someone else achieve their dream. You have done the necessary work and now you have to be patient to allow others to do theirs.

SPLIT GILL

adapt

Schizophyllum commune

EDIBLE / MEDICINAL

You will find the split gill on every continent in the world (except Antarctica) as well as all year round. It grows in sunny places on dead or dying wood, and prefers deciduous trees such as beech, linden alder and oak. It has received its name due to its radial gill-like folds, which are centrally split. These splits allow it to open and close because they dry out with prolonged dry weather and then rehydrate with the rain, many times over a growing period. Another amazing fact is that they have more than 28,000 different sexes, where many species have only four or five. Split gill tends to be quite hard but is still edible and is used in China and Japan for its medicinal qualities. *S. commune* is said to increase energy, enhance the immune system, treat gynaecological issues and be a supportive treatment for cancer.

Card meaning

Being able to adapt to any condition or environment is important. How do you weather the storm? Do you conserve your energy when the time is quiet, and do you notice nature's cycles happening around you? When you become more in tune with your natural surroundings, you understand energy flow. You can choose to align yourself with this energy and ease into a state of flow, or you can fight the cycles and burn out or exhaust yourself by trying to swim up-stream against the current.

The split gill shows you how to adapt to the current situation to preserve yourself. Is there a situation in your life at present that you need to stop fighting and just give in to the flow or adapt to the current circumstances? There may be a situation coming up that you need to adapt to, so remember this advice when it comes. Not everyone will be a fan of what you do, but there are others who will.

There is no pleasing everybody, so just please yourself and do what is necessary to provide yourself with a safe environment.

This also says that you might want to take time out and only re-emerge when you are rested and feeling more refreshed. Maybe taking a break from social media or a situation that has left you feeling deflated is needed. Recharge yourself and only give yourself things that nourish you mentally, emotionally, physically and spiritually. Then when you are fully charged, come back into view.

26

RED CAGE
capture
Clathrus ruber

EDIBLE

(in its egg stage)

The red cage mushroom is another member of the stinkhorn family. The mycelium first grows what looks like an egg, which hatches and then the red cage grows up and out of it. Inside the cage is gleba, a gooey substance that creates a putrid smell flies love. The flies swarm to the cage, eat the gleba, but more importantly, carry the mushroom spores off with them. The cage lasts about 24 hours before collapsing and decomposing. *C. ruber* can reach a whopping 20 centimetres tall!

Card meaning

Go after what you want, but don't hold on too tightly to it. The red cage mushroom is effective at what it does – and that is, it gets what it wants. The holes in the cage are too large to hold anything in, but the gleba is inside, so the flies must go in. The flies don't ever get stuck; they are not trapped, just enticed by what is on offer. They have formed a relationship with the cage mushroom. One of mutual reciprocity.

The message here is to know what is necessary to capture your dreams. Do whatever it takes until you get what you want. Learn what you need to do or acquire to manifest what you want. Do you need to upskill, read and research more; do a course; or ask questions from others? Ask yourself, 'What do I need to do to bring me what I want?' Once you understand what is needed, put your plan in place and execute it. Form the relationships you need and make progress towards your goals. It is only you who can set the trap.

When you capture what you are trying to, let it go. If it can come and go freely, it will set the wheels in motion for the larger purpose you needed for it to manifest. Something that may have seemed frightening at first might reveal to you it is here to help and has a greater purpose than you assumed.

27

BLUE LERATIOMYCES
discovery/unknown

Leratiomyces sp.

UNKNOWN

(most likely inedible)

Blue leratiomyces is a recent find in Australia by Steve Axford, so there is not much information surrounding it yet. It has an unusual shape and beautiful blue colour, with what looks like a dusting of sugar on it.

Card meaning

A new discovery awaits you, and it's going to be like stepping into the unknown, so don't move forward with assumptions of what it's going to be like. Go in with an open mind and heart and allow it to unfold without expectation. Sometimes you are not meant to know what the unknown holds for you, because you need to actually experience it. You may see it as negative; you might find it positive. Either way, know that it is important and exactly where you are meant to be. If things don't turn out the way you thought and you find yourself in a negative thought pattern, remind yourself to give thanks for the situation, even though you are not sure why it may be happening. It will most likely be revealed to you at a later date, because it was a steppingstone for you to get to somewhere else.

If you could see the whole path ahead of you, would you take a step forward? Sometimes it's good not to know where you are heading because the road ahead may be too overwhelming. Take a steppingstone approach and move from one to the next without worrying where they are taking you. As long as you follow your intuition, you won't be led astray. If you are allowing logical and emotional decisions to override your intuitive processes, you will find too many pathways you can take. Intuition is key here. Be strong, be confident and trust your gut. The unknown awaits and it has many gifts for you!

28

MYCENA INTERRUPTA
purpose/judgement
Mycena interrupta

INEDIBLE

M. interrupta, also known as pixie's parasol, is a striking little mushroom, standing up to 22 millimetres high. Don't be fooled by how little and fragile it is – most of its mass is within the wood it is decomposing. Keep in mind the mushroom is simply the fruiting body of the mycelium. It is only found in south-eastern Australia, New Zealand, New Caledonia and Chile, which is known as the Gondwanan distribution. This is because these countries are part of an ancient supercontinent that broke up about 200 million years ago. In Australia, it is known as Gondwanaland. Another rare mushroom, small with big purpose.

Card meaning

A small but mighty mushroom with a big purpose. Don't ever let looks fool you. Remember the analogy of the tip of the iceberg – you never know what's under the surface. You see only what wants or needs to be shown. The mycelium of this mushroom is a mass within the wood, slowly decomposing it and turning it into nutrients that supplies the nearby trees. It is small but plays such an important role. It is not only stunning, but hard to spot because it is a tiny mushroom.

This card indicates that you don't need to be seen while completing your purpose and don't be worried about what people assume about you. Small and fragile does not mean insignificant and useless. It means there is beauty in everything seen and unseen, and not to judge a situation or person at first glance. It takes time to understand any person or thing, because there is always so much more under the surface.

It could also mean not to judge a book by its cover. People have so much more depth to them than they let on. There is always more to learn about a person or situation so don't assume. Gather your information and look deeper.

29

OCTOPUS STINKHORN
reveal
Clathrus archeri

EDIBLE

(but not recommended)

With the nickname devil's fingers, one would think the octopus stinkhorn is a poisonous or deadly mushroom. It seems that the colours and shape of mushrooms don't really tell us if they are poisonous or not. It is sometimes the plain, white-looking ones that you must steer clear of. Being in the stinkhorn family, *C. archeri* is another putrid-smelling mushroom that attracts flies, which redistribute the mushroom spores. Like the red cage mushroom, the octopus stinkhorn erupts from what looks like an egg, with between four to seven arms initially all connected then unfolding outwards and revealing the spore-containing putrid-smelling gleba.

Card meaning

If we have learned anything from mushrooms, it is not to assume or judge them on their appearance. The octopus stinkhorn or devil's fingers is one of these. It is not poisonous or reaching up from the bowels of hell as some would believe. It is just incredibly good at getting what it wants, but that only happens once it fully reveals itself.

Once you reach a certain point in life or with a project, you need to reveal yourself or it to the world for it to serve its purpose. This card is telling you this is what needs to happen. This is a good thing, no matter what it seems to look like. Don't let fear of judgement stand in your way if you know this is what you are meant to do.

This card also may mean that something or someone is going to make a reveal to you. It might be shocking, it may already be foreseen, but don't cast judgement – just allow it to happen as it is meant to. When we peel away the layers to reveal what is underneath, we allow ourselves freedom to be ourselves. Reveal, let go, no judgement. The purpose is far greater than what is on the surface.

30

PARROT WAXCAP
isolation
Gliophorus psittacinus

EDIBLE

(not advised due to its slimy texture;
can also cause gastrointestinal upset)

The parrot waxcap is a striking slimy-green mushroom that can be found growing in autumn on roadside verges and cropped grasslands. It prefers untampered, acidic or neutral soil/grassland and may also grow in association with moss. Often found in lawns and cemeteries, *G. psittacinus* is widespread across the UK and likes to be left alone, so it can be found in places that have little thoroughfare. These mushrooms have no look-alikes, so cannot be easily misidentified.

Card meaning

The parrot waxcap likes to be left alone, and it's easy to understand why. Isolation can be a good thing.

Left untouched by pollution, noise and people, it grows well. So can you if you are left to your own devices. You are capable of growth without 'all the things'. What you thought you needed to survive, might not actually be necessary. You would be surprised how little you really need at all. Sometimes stripping your life down to the bare necessities can show you how you have been living way beyond your means.

Isolation can also be a good thing to clear your mind and strip yourself down to basics. You will be able to hear your own thoughts again, without the constant bombardment of sound, people and energy. When you need peace in your life, sometimes you need to extricate yourself from the situation. Finding peace is so much easier when you have isolated yourself and attend to what you really need. Sometimes peace and simplicity bring the greatest rewards.

If, on the other hand, you are feeling isolated and not in a good place, ask yourself, 'What do I need? What is it that really sustains me and makes me happy?' It's time to ask the tough questions and really get real about it. Only you know what can make you happy and it has to come from the inside. Addictions are often fuelled by unhappiness. When you find something that makes your heart sing and makes you feel alive, you tend to not need your vices as often.

31

VERDIGRIS AGARIC

impress

Stropharia aeruginosa

UNKNOWN

(depends where you are in the world.
Some guidebooks claim 'poisonous',
others claim 'edible')

This mushroom is named verdigris because of its striking green or green-blue colour – a colour not commonly seen in any other mushroom. Found in the UK, Ireland, Europe and North America, *S. aeruginosa* is rare and loves alkaline, humus-rich beech woodland. White scales adorn the younger caps, giving it a similar appearance to the fly agaric mushroom.

Card meaning

You are beautiful and what you are doing is beautiful. You and your purpose need to stand out because you are different, and this is exactly what is needed at this time. It is time to make yourself seen and show the world the beauty you have to offer.

This is a beautiful card to pull, indicating it is something or someone's time to really make an impression. Standing out for being different or unique can be daunting, but rest assured it will be worth it.

What impresses you in others? Are there certain qualities you admire that you could benefit by taking on yourself? Is there someone who could really use a compliment at the moment because they don't fully believe in themselves? Whatever the situation or the person, this card is saying, 'Now is the time. Don't wait any longer.' The world needs more unique and beautiful beings in the world. Be that person, get that project off the ground, or help elevate someone who needs you.

When you stand up and make an impression on someone, it can have a life-changing effect on them. You never know who may be watching in silence and admiring your beauty. You might help someone find their path by watching your journey and seeing how brave you are by standing out and making yourself seen. We never know how long we are here for, so make your life count. Your purpose doesn't need to be a big one – just do it well and stand proud.

32

ROSY BONNET
define
Mycena rosea

POISONOUS
(due to the low levels of muscarine)

Rosy bonnet shares a striking resemblance to lilac bonnet and many find the two indistinguishable. However, there are minor differences – for example, rosy bonnet's stem is lighter than its cap; the stem is also usually thicker at its base than at the top; and the whole mushroom is also a little larger, with a marked raised centre in the cap. *M. rosea* can be found in leaf litter and smells strongly of radish.

Card meaning

There are similarities at play here. Where do you need to look more closely at the finer detail? There is something you might not be noticing and when you understand what you are really looking for, it will be easier to identify. You might be making an assumption about something or someone and aren't really seeing the full picture. Make sure you do your research and due diligence in this matter. Really give it a lot of thought then when you are certain what you need to look for, put it into action.

This card might also mean that you need to help others see what is before them and show them how to look for similarities so they too can find exactly what they are searching for.

It could be a time to define what you are looking for. Are you being a bit too vague and need to really look at the finer details? Only when we truly define what it is that we want, can we manifest it in our lives.

Don't be fooled by appearances either. Someone may be trying to be something they are not. There might not be anything wrong with that, but it is always good to understand why. Not everything is as it seems, but that is not always something to be worried about. Keep your wits about you and see what's really in front of you. Looks can be deceiving.

33

INDIGO MILK CAP
true colours
Lactarius indigo

EDIBLE

This amazing blue mushroom is edible and is said to taste very much like a portobello; however, it will stain everything green. It is blue throughout the entire inside of the mushroom and bleeds a blue milky substance when cut that slowly turns green upon exposure to air. It is quite well spread around the world and likes the soil in oak and pine woodlands. *L. indigo*'s bright blue pigment also has many uses, including as a dye.

Card meaning

Let your true colours shine from within. Some people cannot hide who they are and some never show their true colours. The indigo milk cap is a stunning mushroom. With its distinguishing features, it can't

95

be mistaken for anything else. When you cut it in half, the colour inside is that of the outside. Your internal environment reflects in your external environment and vice versa. You show who you truly are from the inside, and this should be celebrated.

This card may be asking whether someone is showing their true colours or hiding them from view. Do you know your friends inside and out? Do you know yourself inside and out? When you understand yourself fully, it gives you a wealth of information to understand others. Do you see traits in others that are red flags? Always trust your intuition when it comes to people and situations you find yourself in. Your gut tells you when something doesn't add up. Like when someone says one thing and does another. Take notice of these things and the people around you. Do you really need these kinds of influences in your life? You always have options open to you. You can choose to walk away from or confront them.

Remember, masks can only last so long before true colours show through. If it is you who needs to show your true colours, step into your power and do it. The time is here!

34

BLEEDING TOOTH

stagnation

Hydnellum peckii

EDIBLE / MEDICINAL

(however, not generally recommended for consumption due to its bitter taste)

Although it looks like something that could be poisonous, the bleeding tooth fungus is completely safe to eat. The pale flesh cap exudes a deep red liquid that looks like blood and is thought to be a type of sap, due to an excess of water. Underneath, it is covered with small spikes, which produce its spores. When it matures, it turns into a dull brown mushroom. Used to create a beige dye, *H. peckii* is also being researched for its possible medicinal qualities. It tends to be found in old coniferous forests that don't suffer from pollution, and it has a mycorrhizal relationship with the trees, meaning it breaks down nitrogen and phosphorus and passes on all the extra nutrients it doesn't need to its tree host.

Medically, this mushroom contains atromentin, known to be an anti-coagulant that inhibits blood clotting. Also, the flesh contains thelephoric acid, which may be useful for treating Alzheimers. So, does the red sap look like blood clots to you? Or possibly the plaque formation within the brain of an Alzheimers patient? Two fairly prominent doctrine of signatures here, don't you reckon?

Card meaning

Is there stagnation happening somewhere in your life at present? The bleeding tooth card is asking you where you need to shift stagnant energy. It may be in the form of something emotional or physical, or an unfinished project. The question to ask yourself is, 'Why am I allowing this to stagnate? Why do I not want to move on from this?' or 'Why it is so hard for me to look at this?' Is it in the too-hard basket or something you have been avoiding for whatever reason? Whatever it is, don't let it fester. Don't let it go unnoticed because doing so will only create more issues further down the track. Why deal with it then when you can deal with it now and avoid making it any worse?

Sometimes when you truly decide to turn your attention to something, the task isn't as hard as you first thought. Things can move quicker than you can imagine, so let go of the assumptions of what could be or what might happen, and attend to the matter. If it is a difficult matter, sweeping it under the carpet doesn't help anybody. Everything is there to grow from and catapult you to where you are meant to be.

Let the flow begin, and when the stagnation shifts, this creates space for something new and fresh. It creates a harmonious flow, and your tension can ease. Peace always ensues.

35

VIOLET CORAL

community

Clavaria zollingeri

EDIBLE

(but not recommended due to its rarity)

The beautiful violet coral mushroom is rare and small, growing up to 10 centimetres high. *C. zollingeri* likes coniferous woodland and high-quality unimproved grassland. The violet colour fades to a dull brown-grey when old. It will also lose its colour when dried, so its pigment may be light-sensitive.

Card meaning

This is a mushroom that looks like it should be in the sea. Little is known about this rarity, except that it loses its colour when picked and dried. It also changes colour when it is old and dying.

The violet coral card reminds you to be unapologetically you. Be who you are meant to

100

be while you are here and when you depart, your essence will go with you. It doesn't matter if you stand out as being different, someone will always admire you for that. People who truly love you see you for who you are on the inside. Your spirit, your soul essence is what makes you, you. What you learn in each lifetime is carried through to the next and the next, until you are a wise soul who has learned a lot of lessons and accumulated much knowledge during your time on earth.

Do you feel like you are not where you are meant to be? Maybe it is time to assess where you are at and where you need to be. Do you need to find your tribe? Your community? Somewhere you feel you fit in better? If so, start looking. Seek out others like you or with similar interests. If you've always loved the water, maybe it's time to make a sea change? Or is it possible that you are exactly where you are meant to be to make a difference? Rarely do we find ourselves in certain circumstances if we are not meant to learn something. Be true to yourself.

36

Dead man's fingers
timing
Xylaria polymorpha

INEDIBLE

Dead man's fingers may give you a fright if you come upon it, but rest assured, it's harmless. It can grow up to 8 centimetres tall, initially starting off white and maturing to brown or black, while the flesh inside remains white. *X. polymorpha* grows from stumps and buried deadwood and especially loves beech trees. It pokes up through the dead leaves on the ground and moss. Some mushrooms only last for days, but dead man's fingers can last a few years. When its spores are released over a long period, it will eventually find a favourable time.

Card meaning

Timing is the key here. Are you needing to wait until the time is right, or do you try and try again until you achieve the right time? Some things can't be rushed and other things are time sensitive, so if you have the power to control the timing to work in your best interest, do so. If you know when the right time is, wait until then and don't rush in beforehand. Just as you grow seeds into a plant, you can't plant seeds in the wrong season and expect them to grow.

If you're uncertain what the right time is, just keep moving until you do know. If it is important, the right time will appear. Timing is a funny thing, if you wait too long, you can miss the boat, or if you arrive early, you might think the boat has left, but it hasn't come yet. Let your intuition be your guide and let everything unfold in divine timing. Don't push because you are impatient, let it come to you because you are both in vibrational alignment. Look at the reasons around why you might not be achieving something and see what you have to learn from it. Remember, time only exists in the physical realm. You are a limitless being who can transcend time and space. When you learn your lesson, you break patterns and cycles, so if you do the inner work, shifts can happen instantly.

ABOUT THE AUTHOR

Nicola McIntosh is an artist and author of *Plant Spirit Medicine* (Rockpool 2022). She is also a herbalist who practises Celtic shamanism, which gives her a passion for everything botanical and mushroom related. Nicola sees herself as a messenger for the spiritual realm. She is able to bring these messages into her artwork as she has in the *Mushroom Spirit Oracle*. These messages allow you to look within and become your own teacher. She values the importance of self-care and her work is dedicated to raising consciousness through working on one's self for the greater good.

You can follow her work here:
www.spiritstone.com.au